Letters
OF A WOMAN
HOMESTEADER

– PART TWO –

Elinore
Pruitt
Stewal

first published by
THE ATLANTIC
MONTHLY CO.
1913 – 1914

X
THE STORY OF CORA BELLE

August 15, 1910.
Dear Mrs. Coney,—

... Grandma Edmonson's birthday is the 30th of May, and Mrs. O'Shaughnessy suggested that we give her a party. I had never seen Grandma, but because of something that happened in her family years ago which a few narrow-heads whom it didn't concern in the least cannot forgive or forget, I had heard much of her. The family consists of Grandma, Grandpa, and little Cora Belle, who is the sweetest little bud that ever bloomed upon the twigs of folly.

The Edmonsons had only one child, a daughter, who was to have married a man whom her parents objected to solely because he was a sheep-man, while their sympathies were with the cattle-men, although they owned only a small bunch. To gain their consent the young man closed out his interest in sheep, at a loss, filed on a splendid piece of land near them, and built a little home for the girl he loved. Before they could get to town to be married Grandpa was stricken with rheumatism. Grandma was already almost past going on with it, so they postponed the marriage, and as that winter was particularly severe, the young man took charge of the Edmonson stock and kept them from starving. As soon as he was able he went for the license.

Mrs. O'Shaughnessy and a neighbor were hunting some cattle that had wandered away and found the poor fellow shot in the back. He was not yet dead and told them it was urgently necessary for them to hurry him to the Edmonsons' and to get some one to perform the marriage ceremony as quickly as possible, for he could not live long. They told him such haste meant quicker death because he would bleed more; but he insisted, so they got a wagon and hurried all they could. But they could not outrun death. When he knew he could not live to reach home, he asked them to witness all he said. Everything he possessed he left to the girl he was to have married, and said he was the father of the little child that was to come. He begged them to befriend the poor girl he had to leave in such a condition, and to take the marriage license as evidence that he had tried to do right. The wagon was stopped so the jolting would not make death any harder, and there in the shadow of the great twin buttes he died.

They took the body to the little home he

had made, and Mrs. O'Shaughnessy went to the Edmonsons' to do what she could there. Poor Cora Jane didn't know how terrible a thing wounded pride is. She told her parents her misdeeds. They couldn't see that they were in any way to blame. They seemed to care nothing for her terrible sorrow nor for her weakened condition. All they could think of was that the child they had almost worshiped had disgraced them; so they told her to go.

Mrs. O'Shaughnessy took her to the home that had been prepared for her, where the poor body lay. Some way they got through those dark days, and then began the waiting for the little one to come. Poor Cora Jane said she would die then, and that she wanted to die, but she wanted the baby to know it was loved,—she wanted to leave something that should speak of that love when the child should come to understanding. So Mrs. O'Shaughnessy said they would make all its little clothes with every care, and they should tell of the love. Mrs. O'Shaughnessy is the daintiest needleworker I have ever seen; she was taught by the nuns at St. Catherine's in the "ould country." She was all patience with poor, unskilled Cora Jane, and the little outfit that was finally finished was dainty enough for a fairy. Little Cora Belle is so proud of it.

At last the time came and Mrs. O'Shaughnessy went after the parents. Long before, they had repented and were only too glad to go. The poor mother lived one day and night after the baby came. She laid the tiny thing in her mother's arms and told them to call her Cora Belle. She told them she gave them a pure little daughter in place of the sinful one they had lost.

That was almost twelve years ago, and the Edmonsons have lived in the new house all this time. The deed to the place was made out to Cora Belle, and her grandfather is her guardian.....

If you traveled due north from my home, after about nine hours' ride you would come into an open space in the butte lands, and away between two buttes you would see the glimmer of blue water. As you drew nearer you would be able to see the fringe of willows around the lake, and presently a low, red-roofed house with corrals and stables. You would see long lines of "buck" fence, a flock of sheep near by, and cattle scattered about feeding. This is Cora Belle's home. On the long, low porch you would see two old folks rocking. The man is small,

and has rheumatism
in his legs and feet
so badly that he
can barely hobble.
The old lady is
large and fat, and is
also afflicted with
rheumatism, but has
it in her arms and
shoulders. They are
both cheerful and
hopeful, and you
would get a cordial
welcome....

When you saw Cora

Belle you would see a stout, square-built little figure with long flaxen braids, a pair of beautiful brown eyes and the longest and whitest lashes you ever saw, a straight nose, a short upper lip, a broad, full forehead,—the whole face, neither pretty nor ugly, plentifully sown with the brownest freckles. She is very truly the head of the family, doing all the housework and looking after the stock, winter and summer, entirely by herself. Three years ago she took things into her own hands, and since that time has managed altogether. Mrs. O'Shaughnessy, however, tells her what to do.

The sheep, forty in number, are the result of her individual efforts. Mrs. O'Shaughnessy told her there was more money in raising lambs than in raising chickens, so she quit the chickens as a business and went to some of the big sheep-men and got permission to take the "dogie" lambs, which they are glad to give away. She had plenty of cows, so she milked cows and fed lambs all day long all last year. This year she has forty head of nice sheep worth four dollars each, and she doesn't have to feed them the year round as she would chickens, and the wolves are no worse to kill sheep than they are to kill chickens. When shearing-time came she went to a sheep-man and told him she would help cook for his men one week if he would have her sheep sheared with his. She said her work was worth three dollars, that is what one man would get a day shearing, and he could easily shear her sheep in one day. That is how she got her sheep sheared. The man had her wool hauled to town with his, sold it for her, and it brought sixty dollars. She took her money to Mrs. O'Shaughnessy. She wanted some supplies ordered before she went home, because, as she gravely said, "the rheumatiz would get all the money she had left when she got home,"— meaning that her grandparents would spend what remained for medicine.

The poor old grandparents read all the time of wonderful cures that different dopes accomplish, and they spend every nickel they can get their hands on for nostrums.

They try everything they read of, and have to buy it by the case,—horrid patent stuff! They have rolls of testimonials and believe every word, so they keep on trying and hoping. When there is any money they each order whatever medicine they want to try. If Mrs. Edmonson's doesn't seem to help her, Grandpa takes it and she takes his,—that is their idea of economy. They would spend hours telling you about their different remedies and would offer you spoonful after spoonful of vile-looking liquid, and be mildly grieved when you refused to take it. Grandma's hands are so bent and twisted that she can't sew, so dear old Grandpa tries to do it.

Mrs. O'Shaughnessy told me that she helped out when she could. Three years ago she made them all a complete outfit, but the "rheumatiz" has been getting all the spare money since then, so there has been nothing to sew. A peddler sold them a piece of gingham which they made up for Cora Belle. It was broad pink and white stripes, and they wanted some style to "Cory's" clothes, so they cut a gored skirt. But they had no pattern and made the gores by folding a width of the goods biasly and cutting it that way. It was put together with no regard to matching the stripes, and a bias seam came in the center behind, but they put no stay in the seam and the result was the most outrageous affair imaginable.

Well, we had a large room almost empty and Mr. Stewart liked the idea of a party, so Mrs. Louderer, Mrs. O'Shaughnessy, and myself planned for the event. It was to be a sewing-bee, a few good neighbors invited, and all to sew for Grandma.... So Mrs. O'Shaughnessy went to Grandma's and got all the material she had to make up. I had saved some sugar-bags and some flour-bags. I knew Cora Belle needed underwear, so I made her some little petticoats of the larger bags and some drawers of the smaller. I had a small piece of white lawn that I had no use for, and of that I made a dear little sunbonnet with a narrow edging of lace around, and also made a gingham bonnet for her. Two days before the time, came Mrs. Louderer, laden with bundles, and Mrs. O'Shaughnessy, also laden. We had all been thinking of Cora Belle. Mr. Stewart had sent by mail for her a pair of sandals for everyday wear and a nice pair of shoes, also some stockings. Mrs. Louderer brought cloth for three dresses of heavy Dutch calico, and gingham for three aprons. She made them herself and she sews so carefully. She had bought patterns and the little dresses were stylishly made, as well as well made. Mrs. O'Shaughnessy brought a piece of crossbar with a tiny forget-me-not polka dot, and also had goods and embroidery for a suit of underwear. My own poor efforts were already completed when the rest came, so I was free to help them.

Late in the afternoon of the 29th a funny something showed up. Fancy a squeaky, rickety old wagon without a vestige of paint. The tires had come off and had been "set" at home; that is done by heating the tires red-hot and having the rims of the wheels covered with several layers of burlap, or other old rags, well wet; then the red-hot tire is put on and water hurriedly poured on to shrink the iron and to keep the burlap from blazing. Well, whoever had set Cora Belle's tires had forgotten to cut away the surplus burlap, so all the ragtags were merrily waving in the breeze.

Cora Belle's team would bring a smile to the soberest face alive. Sheba is a tall, lanky old mare. Once she was bay in color, but the years have added gray hair until now she is roan. Being so long-legged she strides along at an amazing pace which her mate, Balaam, a little donkey, finds it hard to keep up with. Balaam, like Sheba, is full of years. Once his glossy brown coat was the pride of some Mexican's heart, but time has added to his color also, and now he is blue. His eyes are sunken and dim, his ears no longer stand up in true donkey style, but droop dejectedly. He has to trot his best to keep up with Sheba's slowest stride. About every three miles he balks, but little Cora Belle doesn't call it balking, she says Balaam has stopped to rest, and they sit and wait till he is ready to trot along again. That is the kind of layout which drew up before our door that evening. Cora Belle was driving and she wore her wonderful pink dress which hung down in a peak behind, fully six inches longer than anywhere else. The poor child had no shoes. The winter had tried the last pair to their utmost endurance and the "rheumatiz" had long since got the last dollar, so she came with her chubby little sunburned legs bare. Her poor little scarred feet were clean, her toe-nails full of nicks almost into the quick, broken against rocks when she had been herding her sheep. In the back of the wagon, flat on the bottom, sat Grandma and Grandpa, such bundles of coats and blankets I can't describe. After a great deal of trouble we got them unloaded and into the house. Then Mrs. Louderer entertained them while Mrs. O'Shaughnessy and I prepared supper and got a bath ready for Cora Belle. We had a T-bone steak, mashed potatoes, hominy, hot biscuits and butter,

and stewed prunes.
Their long ride had
made them hungry
and I know they
enjoyed their meal.

After supper Cora
Belle and I washed
the dishes while
Mrs. O'Shaughnessy
laid out the little
clothes. Cora Belle's
clothes were to
be a surprise. The
postmistress here
also keeps a small

store and has ribbon, and when she heard of our plans from Mr. Stewart she sent up a couple of pairs of hair-ribbon for Cora Belle. Soon Mrs. O'Shaughnessy called us, and Cora Belle and I went into the bedroom where she was. I wish you could have seen that child! Poor little neglected thing, she began to cry. She said, "They ain't for me, I know they ain't. Why, it ain't my birthday, it's Granny's." Nevertheless, she had her arms full of them and was clutching them so tightly with her work-worn little hands that we couldn't get them. She sobbed so deeply that Grandma heard her and became alarmed. She hobbled

to the door and
pounded with her
poor twisted hands,
calling all the while,
"Cory, Cory Belle,
what ails you?" She
got so excited that
I opened the door,
but Cora Belle told
her to go away. She
said, "They ain't for
you, Granny, and they
ain't for me either."
...

People here observe

Decoration Day faithfully, and Cora Belle had brought half a wagon-load of iris, which grows wild here. Next morning we were all up early, but Cora Belle's flowers had wilted and she had to gather more, but we all hurried and helped. She said as she was going to see her mother she wanted to wear her prettiest dress, so Gale and Mrs. O'Shaughnessy helped her to get ready. The cemetery is only about two miles away, so we were all down quite early. We were obliged to hurry because others were coming to help sew. Cora Belle went at once to the graves where her parents lie side by side, and began talking to her mother just as though she saw her. "You didn't know me, did you, Mother, with my pretty new things? But I am your little girl, Mamma. I am your little Cora Belle." After she had talked and had turned every way like a proud little bird, she went to work. And, oh, how fast she worked! Both graves were first completely covered with pine boughs. It looked like sod, so closely were the little twigs laid. Next she broke the stems off the iris and scattered the blossoms over, and the effect was very beautiful. Then we hurried home and everybody got busy. The men took Grandpa off to another part of the ranch where they were fanning oats to plant, and kept him all day. That was good for him because then he could be with the men all day and he so seldom has a chance to be with men. Several ladies came and they all made themselves at home and worked like beavers, and we all had a fine time.....

Sedalia was present and almost caused a riot. She says she likes unusual words because they lend distinction to conversation. Well, they do—sometimes. There was another lady present whose children are very gifted musically, but who have the bad name of taking what they want without asking. The mother can neither read nor write, and she is very sensitive about the bad name her children have. While we were all busy some one made a remark about how smart these children were. Sedalia thought that a good time to get in a big word, so she said, "Yes, I have always said Lula was a progeny." Mrs. Hall didn't know what she meant and thought that she was casting reflections on her child's honesty, so with her face scarlet and her eyes blazing she said, "Sedalia Lane, I won't allow you nor nobody else to say my child is a progeny. You can take that back or I will slap you peaked." Sedalia took it back in a hurry, so I guess little Lula Hall is not a progeny.

Every one left about four except Gale, Mrs. O'Shaughnessy, Mrs. Louderer, and the Edmonsons. They had farthest to go, so they stayed over night again. We worked until ten o'clock that night over Grandma's clothes, but everything was thoroughly finished.

Every button was on, every thread-end knotted and clipped, and some tired workers lay down to rest, as did a very happy child and a very thankful old lady.

Every one got away by ten o'clock the next morning. The last I saw of little Cora Belle was when the top of a long slope and Balaam had "stopped to rest." The breeze from the south was playfully fluttering the rags on the wheels. Presently I heard a long "hee-haw, hee-haw," and I knew Balaam had rested and had started.

I have been a very busy woman since I began this letter

to you several days ago. A dear little child has joined the angels. I dressed him and helped to make his casket. There is no minister in this whole country and I could not bear the little broken lily-bud to be just carted away and buried, so I arranged the funeral and conducted the services. I know I am unworthy and in no way fitted for such a mission, but I did my poor best, and if no one else is comforted, I am. I know the message of God's love and care has been told once, anyway, to people who have learned to believe more strongly in hell than in heaven.

Dear friend, I do hope that this New Year

will bring you and yours fuller joys than you have ever known. If I had all the good gifts in my hands you should certainly be blessed.

Your sincere friend, Elinore Rupert Stewart.

XI
ZEBBIE'S STORY

September 1, 1910.
Dear Mrs. Coney,—

It was just a few days after the birthday party and Mrs. O'Shaughnessy was with me again. We were down at the barn looking at some new pigs, when we heard the big corral gates swing shut, so we hastened out to see who it could be so late in the day.

It was Zebbie. He had come on the stage to Burnt Fork and the driver had brought him on here.... There was so much to tell, and he whispered he had something to tell me privately, but that he was too tired then; so after supper I hustled him off to bed....

Next morning ... the men went off to their work and Zebbie and I were left to tell secrets. When he was sure we were alone he took from his trunk a long, flat box. Inside was the most wonderful shirt I have ever seen; it looked like a cross between a nightshirt and a shirt-waist.

It was of homespun linen. The bosom was ruffled and tucked, all done by hand,—such tiny stitches, such patience and skill. Then he handed me an old daguerreotype. I unfastened the little golden hook and inside was a face good to see and to remember. It was dim, yet clear in outline, just as if she were looking out from the mellow twilight of long ago. The sweet, elusive smile,—I couldn't tell where it was, whether it was the mouth or the beautiful eyes that were smiling. All that was visible of her dress was the Dutch collar, just like what is being worn now. It was pinned with an ugly old brooch which Zebbie said was a "breast-pin" he had given her. Under the glass on the other side was a strand of faded hair and a slip of paper. The writing on the paper was so faded it was scarcely readable, but it said: "Pauline Gorley, age 22, 1860."

Next he showed me a note written by Pauline, simply worded, but it held a world of meaning for Zebbie. It said, "I spun and wove this cloth at Adeline's, enough for me a dress and you a shirt, which I made. It is for the wedding, else to be buried in. Yours, Pauline." The shirt, the picture, and the note had waited for him all these years in Mothie's care. And now I will tell you the story.

Long, long ago some one did something to some one else and started a feud. Unfortunately the Gorleys were on one side and the Parkers on the other. That it all happened before either Zebbie or Pauline was born made no difference. A Gorley must hate a Parker always, as also a Parker must hate a Gorley. Pauline was the only girl, and she had a regiment of big brothers who gloried in the warfare and wanted only the slightest pretext to shoot a Parker. So they grew up, and Zebbie often met Pauline at the quiltings and other gatherings at the homes of non-partisans. He remembers her so perfectly and describes her so plainly that I can picture her easily. She had brown eyes and hair. She used to ride about on her sorrel palfrey with her boy Cæsar on behind to open and shut plantation gates. She wore a pink calico sunbonnet, and Zebbie says "she was just like the pink hollyhocks that grew by mother's window."

Isn't that a sweet picture?

Her mother and father were both dead, and she and her brothers lived on their plantation. Zebbie had never dared speak to her until one day he had driven over with his mother and sisters to a dinner given on a neighboring plantation. He was standing outside near the wall, when some one dropped a spray of apple blossoms down upon him from an upper window. He looked up and Pauline was leaning out smiling at him. After that he made it a point to frequent places where he might expect her, and things went so well that presently Cæsar was left at home lest he should tell the brothers. She was a loyal little soul and would not desert, although he urged her to, even promising to go away, "plumb away, clean to Scott County if she would go." She told him that her brothers would go even as far as that to kill him, so that they must wait and hope. Finally Zebbie got tired of waiting, and one day he boldly rode up to the Gorley home and formally asked for Pauline's hand. The bullet he got for his presumption kept him from going to the war with his father and brother when they marched away.

Some time later George Gorley was shot and killed from

ambush, and although
Zebbie had not yet
left his bed the
Gorleys believed he
did it, and one night
Pauline came through
a heavy rainstorm,
with only Cæsar,
to warn Zebbie and
to beg him, for her
sake, to get away as
fast as he could that
night. She pleaded
that she could not
live if he were killed
and could never

marry him if he killed her brothers, so she persuaded him to go while they were all innocent.

Well, he did as she wished and they never saw each other again. He never went home again until last Thanksgiving, and dear little Pauline had been dead for years. She herself had taken her little gifts for

Zebbie to Mothie to keep for him. Some years later she died and was buried in the dress she mentioned. It was woven at Adeline Carter's, one of the bitterest enemies of the Gorleys, but the sacrifice of her pride did her no good because she was long at rest before Zebbie knew. He had been greatly grieved because no stone marked her grave, only a tangle of rose-briers. So he bought a stone, and in the night before Decoration Day he and two of Uncle Buck's grandsons went to the Gorley burying-ground and raised it to the memory of sweet Pauline. Some of the Gorleys still live there, so he came home at once, fearing if they should find out who placed the stone above their sister they would take vengeance on his poor, frail body.

After he had finished telling me his story, I felt just as I used to when Grandmother opened the "big chist" to air her wedding clothes and the dress each of her babies wore when baptized. It seemed almost like smelling the lavender and rose-leaves, and it was with reverent fingers that I folded the shirt, the work of love, yellow with age, and laid it in the box....

Well, Mrs. O'Shaughnessy returned, and early one morning we

started with a wagon and a bulging mess-box for Zebbie's home. We were going a new and longer route in order to take the wagon. Dandelions spread a carpet of gold. Larkspur grew waist-high with its long spikes of blue. The service-bushes and the wild cherries were a mass of white beauty. Meadowlarks and robins and bluebirds twittered and sang from every branch, it almost seemed. A sky of tenderest blue bent over us and fleecy little clouds drifted lazily across.... Soon we came to the pineries, where we traveled up deep gorges and cañons. The sun shot arrows of gold through the pines down upon us and we gathered our arms full of columbines. The little black squirrels barked and chattered saucily as we passed along, and we were all children together. We forgot all about feuds and partings, death and hard times. All we remembered was that God is good and the world is wide and beautiful. We plodded along all day.

Next morning there was a blue haze that Zebbie said meant there would be a high wind, so we hurried to reach his home that evening.

The sun was hanging like a great red ball in the smoky haze when we entered the long cañon in which is Zebbie's cabin. Already it was dusky in the cañons below, but not a breath of air stirred. A more delighted man than Zebbie I never saw when we finally drove up to his low, comfortable cabin. Smoke was slowly rising from the chimney, and Gavotte, the man in charge, rushed out and the hounds set up a joyful barking. Gavotte is a Frenchman, and he was all smiles and gesticulations as he said, "Welcome, welcome! To-day I am rejoice you have come. Yesterday I am despair if you have come because I am scrub, but to-day, behold, I am delight."

I have heard of clean people, but Gavotte is the cleanest man I ever saw. The cabin floor was so white I hated to step upon it. The windows shone, and at each there was a calico curtain, blue-and-white check, unironed but newly washed. In one window was an old brown pitcher, cracked and nicked, filled with thistles. I never thought them pretty before, but the pearly pink and the silvery green were so pretty and looked so clean that they had a new beauty. Above the fireplace was a great black eagle which Gavotte had killed, the wings outspread and a bunch of arrows in the claws. In one corner near the fire was a washstand, and behind it hung the fishing-tackle. Above one door was a gun-rack, on which lay the rifle and shotgun, and over the other door was a pair of deer-antlers. In the center of the room stood the square home-made table, every inch scrubbed. In the side room, which is the bedroom, was a wide bunk made of pine plank that had also been scrubbed, then filled with fresh, sweet pine boughs, and over them was spread a piece of canvas that had once been a wagon sheet, but Gavotte had washed it and boiled and pounded it until it was clean and sweet. That served for a sheet.

Zebbie was beside himself with joy. The hounds sprang upon him and expressed their joy unmistakably. He went at once to the corrals to see the "critters," and every one of them was safely penned for the night. "Old Sime," an old ram (goodness knows how old!), promptly butted him over, but he just beamed with pleasure. "Sime knows me, dinged if he don't!" was his happy exclamation.

We went into the cabin and left him fondling the "critters."

Gavotte did himself proud getting supper. We had trout and the most delicious biscuit. Each of us had a crisp, tender head of lettuce with a spoonful of potato salad in the center. We had preserves made from canned peaches, and the firmest yellow butter. Soon it was quite dark and we had a tiny brass lamp which gave but a feeble light, but it was quite cool so we had a blazing fire which made it light enough.

When supper was over, Zebbie called us out and asked us if we could hear anything. We could hear the most peculiar, long-drawn, sighing wail that steadily grew louder and nearer. I was really frightened, but he said it was the forerunner of the windstorm that would soon strike us. He said it was wind coming down Crag Cañon, and in just a few minutes it struck us like a cold wave and rushed, sighing, on down the cañon. We could hear it after it had passed us, and it was perfectly still around the cabin. Soon we heard the deep roaring of the coming storm, and Zebbie called the hounds in and secured the door. The sparks began to fly up the chimney. Jerrine lay on a bearskin before the fire, and Mrs.

O'Shaughnessy and I sat on the old blue "settle" at one side. Gavotte lay on the other side of the fire on the floor, his hands under his head. Zebbie got out his beloved old fiddle, tuned up, and began playing. Outside the storm was raging, growing worse all the time. Zebbie played and played. The worse the tumult, the harder the storm, the harder he played. I remember I was holding my breath, expecting the house to be blown away every moment, and Zebbie was playing what he called "Bonaparte's Retreat." It all seemed to flash before me—I could see those poor, suffering soldiers staggering along in the snow, sacrifices to one man's unholy ambition. I verily believe we were all bewitched. I shouldn't have been surprised to have seen witches and gnomes come tumbling down the chimney or flying in at the door, riding on the crest of the storm. I glanced at Mrs. O'Shaughnessy. She sat with her chin in her hand, gazing with unseeing eyes into the fire. Zebbie seemed possessed; he couldn't tire.

It seemed like hours had passed and the tumult had not diminished. I felt like shrieking, but I gathered Jerrine up into my arms and carried her in to bed. Mrs. O'Shaughnessy came with us. She touched my elbow and said, "Child, don't look toward the window, the banshees are out to-night." We knelt together beside the bed and said our beads; then, without undressing save pulling off our shoes, we crawled under our blankets and lay on the sweet, clean pine. We were both perfectly worn out, but we could not sleep. There seemed to be hundreds of different noises of the storm, for there are so many cañons, so many crooks and turns, and the great forest too. The wind was shrieking, howling, and roaring all at once. A deep boom announced the fall of some giant of the forest. I finally dozed off even in that terrible din, but Zebbie was not so frenzied as he had been. He was playing "Annie Laurie," and that song has always been a favorite of mine. The storm began gradually to die away and "Annie Laurie" sounded so beautiful. I was thinking of Pauline and, I know, to Zebbie, Annie Laurie and Pauline Gorley are one and the same.

I knew no more until I heard Zebbie call out, "Ho, you sleepy-heads, it's day." Mrs. O'Shaughnessy turned over and said she was still sleepy. My former visit had taught me what beauty the early morning would spread before me, so I dressed hastily and went outdoors. Zebbie called me to go for a little walk. The amber light of the new day was chasing the violet and amethyst shadows down the cañons. It was all more beautiful than I can tell you. On one side the cañon-walls were almost straight up. It looked as if we might step off into a very world of mountains. Soon Old Baldy wore a crown of gleaming gold.

The sun was up. We walked on and soon came to a brook. We were washing our faces in its icy waters when we heard twigs breaking, so we stood perfectly still. From out the undergrowth of birch and willows came a deer with two fawns. They stopped to drink, and nibbled the bushes. But soon they scented strangers, and, looking about with their beautiful, startled eyes, they saw us and away they went like the wind. We saw many great trees uptorn by the storm. High up on the cliffs Zebbie showed me where the eagles built every year.... We turned homeward and sat down upon the trunk of a fallen pine to rest and take another look at the magnificent view. Zebbie was silent, but presently he threw a handful of pebbles down the cañon wall. "I am not sorry Pauline is dead. I have never shed a tear. I know you think that is odd, but I have never wanted to mourn. I am glad that it is as it is. I am happy and at peace because I know she is mine. The little breeze is Pauline's own voice; she had a little caressing way just like the gentlest breeze when it stirs your hair. There is something in everything that brings back Pauline: the beauty of the morning, the song of a bird or the flash of its wings. The flowers look like she did. So I have not lost her, she is mine more than ever. I have always felt so, but was never quite sure until I went back and saw where they laid her. I know people think I am crazy, but I don't care for that. I shall not hate to die. When you get to be as old as I am, child, everything will have a new meaning to you."

At last we slowly walked back to the cabin, and at breakfast Zebbie told of the damage the storm had done. He was so common-place that no one ever would have guessed his strange fancy....

I shall never forget Zebbie as I last saw him. It was the morning we started home. After we left the bench that Zebbie lives on, our road wound down into a deeper cañon. Zebbie had followed us to where a turn in the cañon should hide us from view. I looked back and saw him standing on the cliffs, high above us, the early morning sun turning his snowy hair to gold, the breeze-fingers of Pauline tossing the scanty locks. I shall always remember him so, a living monument to a dead past.

Elinore Stewart.

XII
A CONTENTED COUPLE

October 6, 1911.
Dear Mrs. Coney,—

... I once "heared"
Sedalia Lane
telling some of
her experiences,
and she said she
"surreptitiously stole
along." One day,
when I thought the
coast was clear, I

was surreptitiously examining the contents of the tool-chest with a view toward securing to myself such hammers, saws, and what else I might need in doing some carpentry work I had planned. The tool-chest is kept in the granary; both it and the granary are usually kept locked. Now the "gude mon" has an idea that a "wooman" needs no tools, and the use and misuse of his tools have led to numbers of inter-household wars. I was gloating over my opportunity, and also making the best of it, when a medley of burring Scotch voices brought me to a quick realization that discretion is the better part of valor. So I went into seclusion behind a tall oat-bin. It seemed that two neighbors whom I had never seen were preparing to go to town, and had come to get some tools and to see if the Stewart would lend them each a team. Now Mr. Stewart must be very righteous, because he certainly regardeth his beast, although he doesn't always love his neighbor as himself. He was willing, however, for friends Tam Campbell and Archie McEttrick to use his teams, but he himself would take a lighter rig and go along, so as to see that his horses were properly cared for, and to help out in case of need.

They made their

plans, set the day, and went their ways. As soon as I could, I made myself scarce about the granary and very busy about the house, and, like Josiah Allen, I was in a very "happyfied" state of mind. There is nothing Mr. Stewart likes better than to catch me unprepared for something. I had been wanting to go to town, and he had

said I might go with
him next time he
went, if I was ready
when he was. I knew
I would not hear
one word about the
proposed trip, but
that only added to
the fun. I had plenty
of time to make all
preparations; so the
day before they were
to start found me
with all in readiness.
It was quite early in
the spring and the

evenings were quite chilly. We had just finished supper, when we heard a great rumbling, and I knew neighbors Campbell and McEttrick had arrived on their way to town; so I began to prepare supper for them. I hadn't expected a woman, and was surprised when I saw the largest, most ungainly person I have ever met come shambling toward me.

She was Aggie McEttrick. She is tall and raw-boned, she walks with her toes turned out, she has a most peculiar lurching gait like a camel's. She has skin the color of a new saddle, and the oddest straggly straw-colored hair. She never wears corsets and never makes her waists long enough, so there is always a streak of gray undershirt visible about her waist. Her skirts are never long enough either, and she knits her own stockings. Those inclined can always get a good glimpse of blue-and-white striped hose. She said, "I guess you are the Missus." And

that was every word
she said until I had
supper on the table.
The men were busy
with their teams, and
she sat with her feet
in my oven, eyeing
my every movement.
I told her we had just
had our supper, but
she waited until I had
theirs ready before
she announced
that neither she
nor Archie ate hot
biscuits or steak,

that they didn't take tea for supper, preferred coffee, and that neither of them could eat peaches or honey. So all of my supper was ruled off except the butter and cream. She went down to their wagons and brought up what she wanted, so Tam Campbell was the only one who ate my honey and biscuit.

Tam is just a Scot with an amazingly close fist, and he is very absent-minded. I had met Annie, his wife, and their six children. She told me of his absent-mindedness. Her remedy for his trouble when it came to household needs was to repeat the article two or three times in the list. People out like we are buy a year's supply at a time. So a list of needed things is made up and sent into town. Tam always managed to forget a great many things.

Well, bedtime came. I offered to show them to their room, but Aggie said, "We'll nae sleep in your bed. We'll jest bide in the kitchen." I could not persuade her to change her mind. Tam slept at the barn in order to see after the "beasties," should they need attention during the night. As I was preparing for bed, Aggie thrust her head into my room and announced that she would be up at three o'clock. I am not an early bird, so I thought I would let

Aggie get her own breakfast, and I told her she would find everything in the pantry. As long as I was awake I could hear Archie and Aggie talking, but I could not imagine what about. I didn't know their habits so well as I came to later. Next morning the rumbling of their wagons awakened me, but I turned over and slept until after six.

There are always so many things to do before leaving that it was nine o'clock before we got started. We had only gotten about two miles, when Mr. Stewart remembered he had not locked the granary, so back we trotted. We nooned only a few miles from home. We knew we could not catch the wagons before camping-time unless we drove very hard, so Mr. Stewart said we would go by the Edmonsons' and spend the night there. I enjoy even the memory of that drive through the short spring afternoon,—the warm red sand of the desert; the Wind

River Mountains wrapped in the blue veil of distance; the sparse gray-green sage, ugly in itself, but making complete a beautiful picture; the occasional glimpse we had of shy, beautiful wild creatures. So much happiness can be crowded into so short a time. I was glad, though, when Cora Belle's home became a part of our beautiful picture. It is situated among great red buttes, and there is a blue lake back of the house. Around the lake is a fringe of willows. Their house is a low, rambling affair, with a long, low porch and a red clay roof. Before the house is a cotton-wood tree, its gnarled, storm-twisted branches making it seem to have the "rheumatiz." There is a hop-vine at one end of the porch. It had not come out when we were there, but the dead vine clung hopelessly to its supports.

Little Cora Belle just bubbled with delight, and her grandparents were scarcely better than she. Spring house-cleaning was just finished, and they have company so seldom that they made us feel that we were doing them a favor by stopping. Poor old "Pa" hobbled out to help put the team away, and when they came back, Cora Belle asked me out to help prepare supper, so I left Mr. Stewart with "Granny" and "Pa" to listen to their recitals and to taste their many medicines. Cora Belle is really an excellent housekeeper. Her cooking would surprise many people. Her bread was delicious, and I am sure I never tasted anything better than the roasted leg of lamb she gave us for supper. I am ashamed to tell you how much I ate of her carrot jam. From where I sat I had a splendid view of the sunset across the lake. Speaking of things singly, Wyoming has nothing beautiful to offer. Taken altogether, it is grandly beautiful, and at sunrise and sunset the "heavens declare His glory."

Cora Belle is so animated and so straightforward,

so entirely clean in all her thoughts and actions, that she commands love and respect at one and the same time. After supper her grandfather asked her to sing and play for us. Goodness only knows where they got the funny little old organ that Cora Belle thinks so much of. It has spots all over it of medicine that has been spilled at different times, and it has, as Cora Belle said, lost its voice in spots; but that doesn't set back Cora Belle at all, she plays away just as if it was all right. Some of the keys keep up a mournful whining and groaning, entirely outside of the tune. Cora Belle says they play themselves. After

several "pieces"
had been endured,
"Pa" said, "Play my
piece, Cory Belle";
so we had "Bingen
on the Rhine" played
and sung from A
to izzard. Dear
old "Pa," his pain-
twisted old face just
beamed with pride. I
doubt if heaven will
have for him any
sweeter music than
his "baby's" voice.
Granny's squeaky,

trembly old voice trailed in after Cora Belle's, always a word or two behind. "Tell my friends and companions when they meet and scrouge around"; that is the way they sang it, but no one would have cared for that, if they had noticed with what happy eagerness the two sang together. The grandparents would like to have sat up all night singing and telling of things that happened in bygone days, but poor tired little Cora Belle began to nod, so we retired. As we were preparing for bed it suddenly occurred to Mr. Stewart that I had not been surprised when going to town was mentioned, so he said, "Wooman, how did it happen that you were ready when I was to gae to the toone?" "Oh," I said, "I knew you were going." "Who tell it ye?" "A little bird." "'T was some fool wooman, mayhap." I didn't feel it necessary to enlighten him, and I think he is still wondering how I knew.

Next morning we

were off early, but we didn't come up with the wagons until almost camping-time. The great heavily-loaded wagons were creaking along over the heavy sands. The McEttricks were behind, Aggie's big frame swaying and lurching with every jolt of the wagon. They never travel without their German socks. They are great thick things to wear on the outside of their shoes. As we came up behind them, we could see Aggie's big socks dangling and bobbing beside Archie's from where they were tied on the back part of the wagon. We could hear them talking and see them gesticulating. When we came nearer, we found they were quarreling, and they kept at it as long as I was awake that night. After the men had disposed of their loads, they and Mr. Stewart were going out of town to where a new coal-mine was being opened. I intended to go on the train to Rock Springs to do some shopping. Aggie said she was going also. I suggested that we get a room together, as we would have to wait several hours for the train, but she was suspicious of my motives. She is greatly afraid of being "done," so she told me to get my own room and pay for it. We got into town about three o'clock in the afternoon, and the train left at midnight.

I had gone to my room, and Jerrine and myself were enjoying a good rest after our fatiguing drive, when my door was thrown open and a very angry Aggie strode in. They asked us fifty cents each for our rooms. Aggie paid hers under protest and afterward got to wondering how long she was entitled to its use. She had gone back to the clerk about it, and he had told her for that night only. She argued that she should have her room for a quarter, as she would only use it until midnight. When that failed, she asked for her money back, but the clerk was out of patience and refused her that. Aggie was angry all through. She vowed she was being robbed. After she had berated me soundly for submitting so tamely, she flounced back to her own room, declaring she would get even with the robbers. I had to hurry like everything that night to get myself and Jerrine ready for the train, so I could spare no time for Aggie. She was not at the depot, and Jerrine and I had to go on to Rock Springs without her. It is only a couple of hours from Green River to Rock Springs, so I had a good nap and a late breakfast. I did my shopping and was back at Green River at two that afternoon. The first person I saw was Aggie. She sat in the depot, glowering at everybody. She had a basket of eggs and a pail of butter, which she had been trying to sell. She was waiting for the night train, the only one she could get to Rock Springs. I asked her had she overslept. "No, I didna," she replied. Then, she proceeded to tell me that, as she had paid for a whole night's use of a room, she had stayed to get its use. That it had made her plans miscarry didn't seem to count.

After all our business was attended to, we started for home. The wagons were half a day ahead of us. When we came in sight, we could see Aggie fanning the air with her long arms, and we knew they were quarreling. I remarked that I could not understand how persons who hated each other so could live together. Clyde told me I had much to learn, and said that really he knew of no other couple who were actually so devoted. He said to prove it I should ask Aggie into the buggy with me and he would get in with Archie, and afterwards we would compare notes. He drove up alongside of them, and Aggie seemed glad to make the exchange. As we had the buggy, we drove ahead of the wagons. It seems that Archie and Aggie are each jealous of the other. Archie is as ugly a little monkey as it would be possible to imagine. She bemeaned him until at last I asked her why she didn't leave him, and added that I would not stand such crankiness for one moment. Then she poured out the vials of her wrath upon my head, only I don't think they were vials but barrels.

About sundown we made it to where we intended to camp

and found that Mrs. O'Shaughnessy had established a sheep-camp there, and was out with her herd herself, having only Manny, a Mexican boy she had brought up herself, for a herder. She welcomed us cordially and began supper for our entire bunch. Soon the wagons came, and all was confusion for a few minutes getting the horses put away for the night. Aggie went to her wagon as soon as it stopped and made secure her butter and eggs against a possible raid by Mrs. O'Shaughnessy. Having asked too high a price for them, she had failed to sell them and was taking them back. After supper we were sitting around the fire, Tam going over his account and lamenting that because of his absent-mindedness he had bought a whole hundred pounds of sugar more than he had intended, Aggie and Archie silent for once, pouting I suspect. Clyde smiled across the camp-fire at me and said, "Gin ye had sic a lass as I hae, ye might blither." "Gin ye had sic a mon as mine—" I began, but Mrs. O'Shaughnessy said, "Gin ye had sic a mon as I hae." Then we all three laughed, for we had each heard the same thing, and we knew the McEttricks wouldn't fight each other. They suspected us of laughing at them, for Archie said to

Aggie, "Aggie, lass, is it sport they are making of our love?" "'T is daft they be, Archie, lad; we'll nae mind their blither." She arose and shambled across to Archie and hunkered her big self down beside him. We went to bed and left them peaceable for once.

I am really ashamed of the way I have

treated you, but I know you will forgive me. I am not strong yet, and my eyes are still bothering me, but I hope to be all right soon now, and I promise you a better letter next time. Jerrine is very proud of her necklace. I think they are so nice for children. I can remember how proud I was of mine when I was a child.

Please give your brother our thanks, and tell him his little gift made my little girl very happy.

I am afraid this letter will seem rather jumbled. I still want the address of your friend in Salem or any other. I shall find time to write, and I am not going to let my baby prevent me from having many enjoyable outings. We call our boy Henry Clyde for his father. He is a dear little thing, but he is a lusty yeller for baby's rights.

With much love, Jerrine and her Mamma.

XIII
PROVING UP

October 14, 1911.
Dear Mrs. Coney,—

I think you must be expecting an answer to your letter by now, so I will try to answer as many of your questions as I remember. Your letter has been mislaid. We have been very much rushed all this week.

We had the thresher crew two days. I was busy cooking for them two days before they came, and have been busy ever since cleaning up after them. Clyde has taken the thresher on up the valley to thresh for the neighbors, and all the men have gone along, so the children and I are alone. No, I shall not lose my land, although it will be over two years before I can get a deed to it. The five years in which I am required to "prove up" will have passed by then. I couldn't have held my homestead if Clyde had also been proving up, but he had accomplished that years ago and has his deed, so I am allowed my homestead. Also

I have not yet used
my desert right, so
I am still entitled
to one hundred
and sixty acres
more. I shall file
on that much some
day when I have
sufficient money
of my own earning.
The law requires
a cash payment of
twenty-five cents per
acre at the filing, and
one dollar more per
acre when final proof

is made. I should not have married if Clyde had not promised I should meet all my land difficulties unaided. I wanted the fun and the experience. For that reason I want to earn every cent that goes into my own land and improvements myself. Sometimes I almost have a brain-storm wondering how I am going to do it, but I know I shall succeed; other women have succeeded. I know of several who are now where they can laugh at past trials. Do you know?—I am a firm believer in laughter. I am real superstitious about it. I think if Bad Luck came along, he would take to his heels if some one laughed right loudly.

I think Jerrine must

be born for the law. She always threshes out questions that arise, to her own satisfaction, if to no one else's. She prayed for a long time for her brother; also she prayed for some puppies. The puppies came, but we didn't let her know they were here until they were able to walk. One morning she saw them following their mother, so she danced for joy. When her little brother came she was plainly disappointed. "Mamma," she said, "did God really make the baby?" "Yes, dear." "Then He hasn't treated us fairly, and I should like to know why. The puppies could walk when He finished them; the calves can, too. The pigs can, and the colt, and even the chickens. What is the use of giving us a half-finished baby? He has no hair, and no teeth; he can't walk or talk, nor do anything else but squall and sleep."

After many days she got the question settled. She began right where she left off. "I know, Mamma, why God gave us such a half-finished baby; so he could learn our ways, and no one else's, since he must live with us, and so we could learn to love him. Every time I stand beside his buggy he laughs and then I love him, but I don't love Stella nor Marvin because they laugh. So that is why." Perhaps that is the reason.

Zebbie's kinsfolk have come and taken him back to Yell County. I should not be surprised if he never returned. The Lanes and the Pattersons leave shortly for Idaho, where "our Bobbie" has made some large investments.

I hope to hear from you soon and that

you are enjoying every minute. With much love,

Your friend,
Elinore Stewart.

XIV
THE NEW HOUSE

December 1, 1911.
Dear Mrs. Coney,—

I feel just like visiting to-night, so I am going to "play like" you have come. It is so good to have you to chat with. Please be seated in this low rocker; it is a present to me from the Pattersons and I am very proud of it. I am just back from the Patterson ranch, and they have a dear little boy who came the 20th of November and they call him Robert Lane.

I am sure this room must look familiar to you, for there is so much in it that was once yours. I have two rooms, each fifteen by fifteen, but this one on the south is my "really" room and in it are my treasures. My house faces east and is built up against a side-hill, or should I say hillside? Anyway, they had to excavate quite a lot. I had them dump the dirt right before the house and terrace it smoothly. I have sown my terrace to California poppies,

and around my porch,
which is six feet
wide and thirty long,
I have planted wild
cucumbers.

Every log in my
house is as straight
as a pine can grow.
Each room has a
window and a door
on the east side,
and the south room
has two windows
on the south with
space between for

my heater, which is one of those with a grate front so I can see the fire burn. It is almost as good as a fireplace. The logs are unhewed outside because I like the rough finish, but inside the walls are perfectly square and smooth. The cracks in the walls are snugly filled with "daubing" and then the walls are covered with heavy gray building-paper, which makes the room very warm, and I really like the appearance. I had two rolls of wall-paper with a bold rose pattern. By being very careful I was able to cut out enough of the roses, which are divided in their choice of color as to whether they should be red, yellow, or pink, to make a border about eighteen inches from the ceiling. They brighten up the wall and the gray paper is fine to hang pictures upon. Those you have sent us make our room very attractive. The woodwork is stained a walnut brown, oil finish, and the floor is stained and oiled just like it. In the corners by the stove and before the windows we take our comfort.

From some broken bamboo fishing-rods I made frames for two screens. These I painted black with some paint that was left from the buggy, and Gavotte fixed the screens so they will stay balanced, and put in casters for me. I had a piece of blue curtain calico

and with brass-
headed tacks I put
it on the frame of
Jerrine's screen, then
I mixed some paste
and let her decorate
it to suit herself
on the side that
should be next her
corner. She used the
cards you sent her.
Some of the people
have a suspiciously
tottering appearance,
perhaps not so very
artistic, but they all

mean something to a little girl whose small fingers worked patiently to attain satisfactory results. She has a set of shelves on which her treasures of china are arranged. On the floor is a rug made of two goatskins dyed black, a present from Gavotte, who heard her admiring Zebbie's bearskin. She has a tiny red rocking-chair which she has outgrown, but her rather dilapidated family of dolls use it for an automobile. For a seat for herself she has a small hassock that you gave me, and behind the blue screen is a world apart.

My screen is made just like Jerrine's except that the cover is cream material with sprays of wild roses over it. In my corner I have a cot made up like a couch. One of my pillows is covered with some checked gingham that "Dawsie" cross-stitched for me. I have a cabinet bookcase made from an old walnut bedstead that was a relic of the Mountain Meadow Massacre. Gavotte made it for me. In it I have my few books, some odds and ends of china, all gifts, and a few fossil curios. For a floor-covering I have a braided rug of blue and white, made from old sheets and Jerrine's old dresses. In the center of my room is a square table made of pine and stained brown. Over it is a table-cover that you gave me. Against the wall near my bed is my "dresser." It is a box with shelves and is covered with the same material as my screen. Above it I have a mirror, but it makes ugly faces at me every time I look into it. Upon the wall near by is a match-holder that you gave me. It is the heads of two fisher-folk. The man has lost his nose, but the old lady still thrusts out her tongue. The material on my screen and "dresser" I bought for curtains, then decided to use some white crossbar I had. But I wish I had not, for every time I look at them I think of poor little Mary Ann Parker.

I am going to make you a cup of tea and

wonder if you will see anything familiar about the teapot. You should, I think, for it is another of your many gifts to me. Now I feel that you have a fairly good idea of what my house looks like, on the inside anyway. The magazines and Jerrine's cards and Mother Goose book came long ago, and Jerrine and I were both made happy. I wish I could do nice things for you, but all I can do is to love you.

Your sincere friend, Elinore Rupert.

XV
THE "STOCKING-LEG" DINNER

February, 1912.
Dear Mrs. Coney,—

... This time I want
to tell you about a
"stocking-leg" dinner
which I attended
not long ago. It
doesn't sound very
respectable, but
it was one of the
happiest events I

ever remember.

Mrs. Louderer was here visiting us, and one afternoon we were all in the kitchen when Gavotte came skimming along on the first pair of snowshoes I ever saw. We have had lots of snow this winter, and many of the hollows and gullies are packed full. Gavotte had no difficulty in coming, and he had come for the mail and to invite us to a feast of "ze hose." I could not think what kind of a dinner it could be, and I did not believe that Mr. Stewart would go, but after Gavotte had explained how much easier it was now than at any other time because the hard-packed

snow made it possible
to go with bobsleds,
I knew he would
go. I can't say I
really wanted to go,
but Mrs. Louderer
took it for granted
that it would be
delightful, so she
and Mr. Stewart did
the planning. Next
morning Gavotte met
Mrs. O'Shaughnessy
and invited her. Then,
taking the mail,
he went on ahead

to blaze a trail we should follow with the sleds. We were to start two days later. They planned we could easily make the trip in a day, as, with the gulches filled with snow, short cuts were possible, and we could travel at a good pace, as we would have a strong team. To me it seemed dangerous, but dinner-parties have not been so plenty that I could miss one. So, when the day came on which we were to start, we were up betimes and had a mess-box packed and Mr. Stewart had a big pile of rocks hot. We all wore our warmest clothes, and the rest carried out hot rocks and blankets while I put the kitchen in such order that the men left to feed the stock would have no trouble in getting their meals. Mr. Stewart carried out the mess-box, and presently we were off. We had a wagon-box on bobsleds, and the box was filled with hay and hot rocks with blankets on top and more to cover us. Mr. Stewart had two big bags of grain in front, feed for the horses, and he sat on them.

It was a beautiful day and we jogged along merrily. We had lots of fun, and as we went a new way, there was much that was new to Mrs. O'Shaughnessy and myself, and it was all new to the rest. Gavotte had told us where we should noon, and we reached the place shortly after twelve. Mr. Stewart went to lift out the mess-box,—but he had forgotten to put it in! Oh, dear! We were a disappointed lot. I don't think I was ever so hungry, but there was nothing for it but to grin and bear it. It did me some good, though, to remember how a man misses his dinner. The horses had to be fed, so we walked about while they were eating. We went up a cañon that had high cliffs on one side, and came to a place where, high up on the rock wall, in great black letters, was this legend: "Dick fell off of this here clift and died." I should think there would be no question that any one who fell from that place on to the boulders below would die.

Soon we started again, and if not quite so jolly as we were before, at least we looked forward to our supper with a keen relish and the horses were urged faster than they otherwise would have been. The beautiful snow is rather depressing, however, when there is snow everywhere. The afternoon passed swiftly and the horses were becoming jaded. At four o'clock it was almost dark. We had been going up a deep cañon and came upon an appalling sight. There had been a snow-slide and the

cañon was half-filled
with snow, rock,
and broken trees.
The whole way was
blocked, and what
to do we didn't
know, for the horses
could hardly be
gotten along and we
could not pass the
snow-slide. We were
twenty-five miles
from home, night
was almost upon us,
and we were almost
starved. But we were

afraid to stay in that cañon lest more snow should slide and bury us, so sadly we turned back to find as comfortable a place as we could to spend the night. The prospects were very discouraging, and I am afraid we were all near tears, when suddenly there came upon the cold air a clear blast from a horn. Mrs.

Louderer cried, "Ach, der reveille!" Once I heard a lecturer tell of climbing the Matterhorn and the calls we heard brought his story to mind. No music could have been so beautiful. It soon became apparent that we were being signaled; so we drove in the direction of the sound and found ourselves going up a wide cañon. We had passed the mouth of it shortly before we had come to the slide. Even the tired horses took new courage, and every few moments a sweet, clear call put new heart into us. Soon we saw a light. We had to drive very slowly and in places barely crept. The bugler changed his notes and we knew

he was wondering if
we were coming, so
Mr. Stewart helloed.
At once we had an
answer, and after
that we were steadily
guided by the horn.
Many times we could
not see the light, but
we drove in the right
direction because we
could hear the horn.

At last, when it was
quite dark and the
horses could go no

farther, we drew up before the fire that had been our beacon light. It was a bonfire built out upon a point of rock at the end of the cañon. Back from it among the pines was a 'dobe house. A dried-up mummy of a man advanced from the fire to meet us, explaining that he had seen us through his field-glasses and, knowing about the snow-slide, had ventured to attract us to his poor place. Carlota Juanita was within, prepared for the señoras, if they would but walk in. If they would! More dead than alive, we scrambled out, cold-stiffened and hungry. Carlota Juanita threw open the low, wide door and we stumbled into comfort. She hastened to help us off with our wraps, piled more wood on the open fire, and busied herself to make us welcome and comfortable. Poor Carlota Juanita! Perhaps you think she was some slender, limpid-eyed, olive-cheeked beauty. She was fat and forty, but not fair. She had the biggest wad of hair that I ever saw, and her face was so fat that her eyes looked beady. She wore an old heelless pair of slippers or sandals that would hardly stay on, and at every step they made the most exasperating sliding noise, but she was all kindness and made us feel very welcome. The floor was of dirt, and they had the largest fireplace I have ever seen, with the widest, cleanest hearth, which was where they did their cooking. All their furniture was home-made, and on a low bench near the door were three water-jars which, I am sure, were handmade. Away back in a corner they had a small altar, on which was a little statue of Mary and the Child.

Before it, suspended by a wire from the rafters, was a cow's horn in which a piece of punk was burning, just as the incense is kept burning in churches. Supper was already prepared and was simmering and smoking on the hearth. As soon as the men came in, Carlota Juanita put it on the table, which was bare of cloth. I can't say that I really like Mexican bread, but they certainly know how to cook meat. They had a most wonderful pot-roast with potatoes and corn dumplings that were delicious. The roast had been slashed in places and small bits of garlic, pepper, bacon, and, I think, parsley, inserted. After it and the potatoes and the dumplings were done, Carlota had poured in a can of tomatoes. You may not think that was good, but I can assure you it was and that we did ample justice to it. After we had eaten until we were hardly able to swallow, Carlota Juanita served a queer Mexican pie. It was made of dried buffalo-berries, stewed and made very sweet. A layer of batter had been poured into a deep baking-dish, then the berries, and then more batter. Then it was baked and served hot with plenty of hard sauce; and it was powerful good, too. She had very peculiar coffee with goat's milk in it. I took mine without the milk, but I couldn't make up my mind that I liked the coffee. We sat around the fire drinking it, when Manuel Pedro Felipe told us it was some he had brought from Mexico. I didn't know they raised it there, but he told us many interesting things about it. He and Carlota Juanita both spoke fairly good

English. They had lived for many years in their present home and had some sheep, a few goats, a cow or two, a few pigs, and chickens and turkeys. They had a small patch of land that Carlota Juanita tilled and on which was raised the squaw corn that hung in bunches from the rafters. Down where we live we can't get sweet corn to mature, but here, so much higher up, they have a sheltered little nook where they are able to raise many things. Upon a long shelf above the fire was an ugly old stone image, the bottom broken off and some plaster applied to make it set level. The ugly thing they had brought with them from some old ruined temple in Mexico. We were all so very tired that soon Carlota Juanita brought out an armful of the thickest, brightest rugs and spread them over the floor for us to sleep upon. The men retired to a lean-to room, where they slept, but not before Manuel Pedro Felipe and Carlota had knelt before their altar for their devotions. Mrs. O'Shaughnessy and myself and Jerrine, knowing the rosary, surprised them by kneeling with them. It is good to meet with kindred faith away off in the mountains. It seems there could not possibly be a mistake when people so far away from creeds and doctrines hold to the faith of their childhood and find the practice a pleasure after so many years. The men bade us good-night, and we lost no time in settling ourselves to rest. Luckily we had plenty of blankets.

Away in the night I was awakened by a noise that frightened me. All was still, but instantly there flashed through my mind tales of murdered travelers, and I was almost paralyzed with fear when again I heard that stealthy, sliding noise, just like Carlota Juanita's old slippers. The fire had burned down, but just then the moon came from behind a cloud and shone through the window upon Carlota Juanita, who was asleep with her mouth open. I could also see a pine bough which was scraping against the wall outside, which was perhaps making the noise. I turned over and saw the punk burning, which cast a dim light over the serene face of the Blessed Virgin, so all fear vanished and I slept as long as they would let me in the morning. After a breakfast of tortillas, cheese, and rancid butter, and some more of the coffee, we started again for the stocking-leg dinner. Carlota Juanita stood in the door, waving to us as long as we could see her, and Manuel P.F. sat with Mr. Stewart to guide us around the snow-slide. Under one arm he carried the horn with which he had called us to him. It came from some long-horned cow in Mexico, was beautifully polished, and had a fancy rim of silver. I should like to own it, but I could not make it produce a sound. When we were safe on our way our guide left us, and our spirits ran high again. The horses were feeling good also, so it was a merry, laughing party that drew up before Zebbie's two hours later.

Long before I had lent Gavotte a set of the Leather-Stocking Tales, which he had read aloud to Zebbie. Together they had planned a Leather-Stocking dinner, at which should be served as many of the viands mentioned in the Tales as possible. We stayed two days and it was one long feast. We had venison served in half a dozen different ways. We had antelope; we had porcupine, or hedgehog, as Pathfinder called it; and also we had beaver-tail, which he found toothsome, but which I did not. We had grouse and sage hen. They broke the ice and snared a lot of trout. In their cellar they had a barrel of trout prepared exactly like mackerel, and they were more delicious than mackerel because they were finer-grained. I had been a little disappointed in Zebbie after his return from home. It seemed to me that

Pauline had spoiled him. I guess I was jealous. This time he was the same little old Zebbie I had first seen. He seemed to thoroughly enjoy our visit, and I am sure we each had the time of our lives. We made it home without mishap the same day we started, all of us sure life held something new and enjoyable after all.

If nothing happens there are some more good times in store for me this summer. Gavotte once worked under Professor Marsden when he was out here getting fossils for the Smithsonian Institution, and he is very interesting to listen to. He has invited us to go with him out to the Bad-Land hills in the summer to search for fossils. The hills are only a few miles from here and I look forward to a splendid time.

XVI
THE HORSE-THIEVES

[No date.]
Dear Mrs. Coney,—

... I am so afraid that you will get an overdose of culture from your visit to the Hub and am sending you an antidote of our sage, sand, and sunshine.

Mrs. Louderer had come over to see

our boy. Together we had prepared supper and were waiting for Clyde, who had gone to the post-office. Soon he came, and after the usual friendly wrangling between him and Mrs. Louderer we had supper. Then they began their inevitable game of cribbage, while I sat near the fire with Baby on my lap. Clyde was telling us of a raid on a ranch about seventy-five miles away, in which the thieves had driven off thirty head of fine horses. There were only two of the thieves, and the sheriff with a large posse was pursuing them and forcing every man they came across into the chase, and a regular man-hunt was on. It was interesting only because one of the thieves was a noted outlaw then out on parole and known to be desperate. We were in no way alarmed; the trouble was all in the next county, and somehow that always seems so far away. We knew if the men ever came together there would be a pitched battle, with bloodshed and death, but there seemed little chance that the sheriff would ever overtake the men.

I remember I was feeling sorry for the poor fellows with a price on their heads,—the little pink man on my lap had softened my heart wonderfully. Jerrine was enjoying the pictures in a paper illustrating early days on the range, wild scenes of roping and branding. I had remarked that I didn't believe there were any more such times, when Mrs Louderer replied, "Dot yust shows how much it iss you do not know. You shall come to mine house and when away you come it shall be wiser as when you left." I had kept at home very closely all summer, and a little trip seemed the most desirable thing I could think of, particularly as the baby would be in no way endangered. But long ago I learned that the quickest way to get what I want is not to want it, outwardly, at least. So I assumed an indifference that was not very real.

The result was that next morning every one was in a hurry to get me started,— Clyde greasing the little old wagon that looks like a twin to Cora Belle's, and Mrs. Louderer, who thinks no baby can be properly brought up without goose-grease, busy greasing the baby "so as he shall not some cold take yet."

Mrs. Louderer had ridden over, so her saddle was laid in the wagon and her pony, Bismarck, was hitched in with Chub, the laziest horse in all Wyoming. I knew Clyde could manage very well while I should be gone, and there wasn't a worry to interfere with the pleasure of my outing.

We jogged along right merrily, Mrs. Louderer devoting her entire attention to trying to make Chub pull even with Bismarck, Jerrine and myself enjoying the ever-changing views. I wish I could lay it all before you. Summer was departing with reluctant feet, unafraid of Winter's messengers, the chill winds. That day was especially beautiful. The gleaming snow peaks and heavy forest south and at our back; west, north, and east, long, broken lines of the distant mountains with their blue haze. Pilot Butte to the north, one hundred miles away, stood out clear and distinct as though we could drive there in an hour or two. The dull, neutral-colored "Bad Land" hills nearer us are interesting only because we know they are full of the fossil remains of strange creatures long since extinct.

For a distance our way lay up Henry's Fork valley; prosperous little ranches dotted the view, ripening grain rustled pleasantly in the warm morning sunshine, and closely cut alfalfa fields made bright spots of emerald against the dun landscape. The quaking aspens were just beginning to turn yellow; everywhere purple asters were a blaze of glory except where the rabbit-bush grew in clumps, waving its feathery plumes of gold. Over it all the sky was so deeply blue, with little, airy, white clouds drifting lazily along. Every breeze brought scents of cedar, pine, and sage. At this point the road wound along the base of cedar hills; some magpies were holding a noisy caucus among the trees, a pair of bluebirds twittered excitedly upon a fence, and high overhead a great black eagle soared. All was so peaceful that horse-thieves and desperate men seemed too remote to think about.

Presently we crossed the creek and headed our course due north toward the desert and the buttes. I saw that we were not going right to reach Mrs.

Louderer's ranch, so I asked where we were supposed to be going. "We iss going to the mouth of Dry Creek by, where it goes Black's Fork into. Dere mine punchers holdts five huntert steers. We shall de camp visit and you shall come back wiser as when you went."

Well, we both came away wiser. I had

thought we were going only to the Louderer ranch, so I put up no lunch, and there was nothing for the horses either. But it was too beautiful a time to let such things annoy us. Anyway, we expected to reach camp just after noon, so a little delay about dinner didn't seem so bad. We had entered the desert by noon; the warm, red sands fell away from the wheels with soft, hissing sounds. Occasionally a little horned toad sped panting along before us, suddenly darting aside to watch with bright, cunning eyes as we passed. Some one had placed a buffalo's skull beside a big bunch of sage and on the sage a splendid pair of elk's antlers. We saw many such scattered over the sands, grim reminders of a past forever gone.

About three o'clock we reached our destination, but no camp was there. We were more disappointed than I can tell you, but Mrs. Louderer merely went down to the river, a few yards away, and cut an armful of willow sticks wherewith to coax Chub to a little brisker pace, and then we took the trail of the departed mess-wagon. Shortly, we topped a low range of hills, and beyond, in a cuplike valley, was the herd of sleek beauties feeding contentedly on the lush green grass. I suppose it sounds odd to hear desert and river in the same breath, but within a few feet of the river the desert begins, where nothing grows but sage and greasewood. In oasis-like spots will be found plenty of grass where the soil is nearer the surface and where sub-irrigation keeps the roots watered. In one of these spots the herd was being held. When the grass became short they would be moved to another such place.

It required, altogether, fifteen men to take care of the herd, because many of the cattle had been bought in different places, some in Utah, and these were always trying to run away

and work back
toward home, so they
required constant
herding. Soon we
caught the glimmer
of white canvas,
and knew it was
the cover of the
mess-wagon, so we
headed that way.

The camp was quite
near the river so
as to be handy to
water and to have
the willows for wood.

Not a soul was at camp. The fire was out, and even the ashes had blown away. The mess-box was locked and Mrs. Louderer's loud calls brought only echoes from the high rock walls across the river. However, there was nothing to do but to make the best of it, so we tethered the horses and went down to the river to relieve ourselves of the dust that seemed determined to unite with the dust that we were made of. Mrs. Louderer declared she was "so mat as nodings and would fire dot Herman so soon as she could see him alreaty."

Presently we saw the most grotesque figure approaching camp. It was Herman, the fat cook, on Hunks, a gaunt, ugly old horse, whose days of usefulness under the saddle were past and who had degenerated into a workhorse. The disgrace of it seemed to be driving him into a decline, but he stumbled along bravely under his heavy load. A string of a dozen sage chickens swung on one side, and across the saddle in front of Herman lay a young antelope. A volley of German abuse was hurled at poor Herman, wound up in as plain American as Mrs. Louderer could speak: "And who iss going to pay de game warden de fine of dot antelope what you haf shot? And how iss it that we haf come de camp by und so starved as we iss hungry, and no cook und no food? Iss dat for why you iss paid?"

Herman was some Dutch himself, however. "How iss it," he demanded, "dat you haf not so much sense as you haf tongue? How haf you lived so long as always in de West und don't

know enough to hunt
a bean-hole when
you reach your own
camp. Hey?"

Mrs. Louderer
was very properly
subdued and I
delighted when he
removed the stones
from where the fire
had been, exposing a
pit from which, with
a pair of pot-hooks,
he lifted pots and
ovens of the most

delicious meat, beans, and potatoes. From the mess-box he brought bread and apricot pie. From a near-by spring he brought us a bright, new pail full of clear, sparkling water, but Mrs. Louderer insisted upon tea and in a short time he had it ready for us. The tarpaulin was spread on the ground for us to eat from, and soon we were showing an astonished cook just how much food two women and a child could get away with. I ate a good deal of ashes with my roast beef and we all ate more or less sand, but fastidiousness about food is a good thing to get rid of when you come West to camp.

When the regular

supper-time arrived the punchers began to gather in, and the "boss," who had been to town about some business, came in and brought back the news of the man-hunt. The punchers sat about the fire, eating hungrily from their tin plates and eagerly listening to the recital. Two of the boys were tenderfeet: one from Tennessee called "Daisy Belle," because he whistled that tune so much and because he had nose-bleed so much,—couldn't even ride a broncho but his nose would bleed for hours afterwards; and the other, "N'Yawk," so called from his native State. N'Yawk was a great boaster; said he wasn't afraid of no durned outlaw,—said his father had waded in bloody gore up to his neck and that he was a chip off the old block,—rather hoped the chase would come our way so he could try his marksmanship.

The air began
to grow chill
and the sky was
becoming overcast.

Preparations for the night busied everybody. Fresh ponies were being saddled for the night relief, the hard-ridden, tired ones that had been used that day being turned loose to graze. Some poles were set up and a tarpaulin arranged for Mrs. Louderer and me to sleep under. Mrs. Louderer and

Jerrine lay down on some blankets and I unrolled some more, which I was glad to notice were clean, for Baby and myself. I can't remember ever being more tired and sleepy, but I couldn't go to sleep. I could hear the boss giving orders in quick, decisive tones. I could hear the punchers discussing the raid, finally each of them telling exploits of his favorite heroes of outlawry. I could hear Herman, busy among his pots and pans. Then he mounted the tongue of the mess-wagon and called out, "We haf for breakfast cackle-berries, first vot iss come iss served, und those vot iss sleep late gets nodings."

I had never before

heard of cackle-berries and asked sleepy Mrs. Louderer what they were. "Vait until morning and you shall see," was all the information that I received.

Soon a gentle, drizzling rain began, and the punchers hurriedly made their beds, as they did so twitting N'Yawk about making his between our tent and the fire. "You're dead right, pard," I heard one of them say, "to make your bed there, fer if them outlaws comes this way they'll think you air one of the women and they won't shoot you. Just us men air in danger."

"Confound your fool tongues, how they goin' to know there's

any women here? I tell you, fellers, my old man waded in bloody gore up to his neck and I'm just like him."

They kept up this friendly parleying until I dozed off to sleep, but I couldn't stay asleep. I don't think I was afraid, but I certainly was nervous. The river was making a sad, moaning sound; the rain fell gently, like tears. All nature seemed to be mourning about something, happened or going to happen. Down by the river an owl hooted dismally. Half a mile away the night-herders were riding round and round the herd. One of them was singing,—faint but distinct came his song: "Bury me not on the lone prairie." Over and over again he sang it. After a short interval of silence he began again. This time it was, "I'm thinking of my dear old mother, ten thousand miles away."

Two punchers stirred uneasily and began talking. "Blast that Tex," I heard one of them say, "he certainly has it bad to-night. What the deuce makes him sing so much? I feel like bawling like a kid; I wish he'd shut up." "He's homesick; I guess we all are too, but they ain't no use staying awake and letting it soak in. Shake the water off the tarp, you air lettin' water catch on your side an' it's running into my ear."

That is the last I heard for a long time. I must have slept. I remember that the baby stirred and I spoke to him. It seemed to me that something struck against the guy-rope that held our tarpaulin taut, but I wasn't sure. I was in that dozy state, half asleep, when

nothing is quite clear.
It seemed as though
I had been listening
to the tramp of
feet for hours and
that a whole army
must be filing past,
when I was brought
suddenly into keen
consciousness
by a loud voice
demanding, "Hello!
Whose outfit is
this?" "This is the
7 Up,—Louderer's,"
the boss called back;

"what's wanted?" "Is that you, Mat? This is Ward's posse. We been after Meeks and Murdock all night. It's so durned dark we can't see, but we got to keep going; their horses are about played. We changed at Hadley's, but we ain't had a bite to eat and we got to search your camp." "Sure thing," the boss answered, "roll off and take a look. Hi, there, you Herm, get out of there and fix these fellers something to eat."

We were surrounded. I could hear the clanking of spurs and the sound of the wet, tired horses shaking themselves and rattling the saddles on every side. "Who's in the wickiup?" I heard the sheriff ask. "Some women and kids,— Mrs. Louderer and a friend."

In an incredibly short time Herman had a fire coaxed into a blaze and Mat Watson and the sheriff went from bed to bed with a lantern. They searched the mess-wagon, even, although Herman had been sleeping there. The sheriff unceremoniously flung out the wood and kindling the cook had stored there. He threw back the flap of our tent and flashed the lantern about. He could see plainly enough that there were but the four of us, but I wondered how they saw outside where the rain made it worse, the lantern was so dirty. "Yes," I heard the sheriff say, "we've been pushing them hard. They're headed north, evidently intend to hit the railroad but they'll never make it. Every ford on the river is guarded except right along here, and there's five parties ranging on the other side. My party's split,—a bunch has gone on to the bridge. If they find anything they're to fire a volley. Same with us. I knew they couldn't cross the river nowhere but at the bridge or here."

The men had gathered about the fire and were gulping hot coffee and cold beef and bread. The rain ran off their slickers in little rivulets. I was sorry the fire was not better, because some of the men had on only ordinary coats, and the drizzling rain seemed determined that the fire should not blaze high.

Before they had finished eating we heard a shot, followed by a regular medley of dull booms. The men were in their saddles and gone in less time than it takes to tell it. The firing had ceased save for a few sharp reports from the revolvers, like a coyote's spiteful snapping. The pounding of the horse's hoofs grew fainter, and soon all was still. I kept my ears strained for the slightest sound. The cook and the boss, the only men up, hurried back to bed. Watson had risen so hurriedly that he had not been careful about his "tarp" and water had run into his bed. But that wouldn't disconcert anybody but a tenderfoot. I kept waiting in tense silence to hear them come back with dead or wounded, but there was not a sound. The rain had stopped. Mrs. Louderer struck a match and said it was three o'clock. Soon she was asleep. Through a rift in the clouds a star peeped out. I could smell the wet sage and the sand. A little breeze came by, bringing Tex's song once more:—

"Oh, it matters not, so I've been told,

How the body lies when the heart grows cold."
Oh, dear! the world seemed so full of sadness. I kissed my baby's little downy head and went to sleep.

It seems that cowboys are rather sleepy-headed in the morning and it is a part of the cook's job to get them up. The next I knew, Herman had a tin pan on which he was beating a vigorous tattoo, all the time hollering, "We haf cackle-berries und antelope steak for breakfast." The baby was startled by the noise, so I attended to him and then dressed myself for breakfast. I went down to the little spring to wash my face. The morning was lowering and gray, but a wind had sprung up and the clouds were parting. There are times when anticipation is a great deal better than realization. Never having seen a cackle-berry, my imagination pictured them as some very luscious wild fruit, and I was so afraid none would be left that I couldn't wait until the men should eat and be gone. So I surprised them by joining the very earliest about the fire. Herman began serving breakfast. I held out my tin plate and received some of the steak, an egg, and two delicious biscuits. We had our coffee in big enameled cups, without sugar or cream, but it was piping hot and so good. I had finished my egg and steak and so I told Herman I was ready for my cackle-berries.

"Listen to her now, will you?" he asked. And then indignantly, "How many cackle-berries does you want? You haf had so many as I haf cooked for you." "Why, Herman, I haven't had a single berry,"

I said. Then such
a roar of laughter.
Herman gazed at me
in astonishment, and
Mr. Watson gently
explained to me that
eggs and cackle-
berries were one and
the same.

N'Yawk was not
yet up, so Herman
walked over to his
bed, kicked him a few
times, and told him
he would scald him

if he didn't turn out. It was quite light by then. N'Yawk joined us in a few minutes. "What the deuce was you fellers kicking up such a rumpus fer last night?" he asked. "You blamed blockhead, don't you know?" the boss answered. "Why, the sheriff searched this camp last night. They had a battle down at the bridge afterwards and either they are all killed or else no one is hurt. They would have been here otherwise. Ward took a shot at them once yesterday, but I guess he didn't hit; the men got away, anyway. And durn your sleepy head! you just lay there and snored. Well, I'll be danged!" Words failed him, his wonder and disgust were so great.

N'Yawk turned to get his breakfast. His light shirt was blood-stained in the back,—seemed to be soaked. "What's the matter with your shirt, it's soaked with blood?" some one asked. "Then that durned Daisy Belle has been crawling in with me, that's all," he said. "Blame his bleeding snoot. I'll punch it and give it something to bleed for."

Then Mr. Watson said, "Daisy ain't been in all night. He took Jesse's place when he went to town after supper." That started an inquiry and search which speedily showed that some one with a bleeding wound had gotten in with N'Yawk. It also developed that Mr. Watson's splendid horse and saddle were gone, the rope that the horse had been picketed with lying just as it had been cut from his neck.

Now all was bustle and excitement. It was plainly evident that one of the outlaws had lain hidden on N'Yawk's bed while the sheriff was there, and that afterwards he had saddled the horse and made his escape. His own horse was found in the willows, the saddle cut loose and the bridle off, but the poor, jaded thing had never moved. By sunup the search-party returned, all too worn-out with twenty-four hours in the saddle to continue the hunt. They were even too worn-out to eat, but flung themselves down for a few hours' rest. The chase was hopeless anyway, for the search-party had gone north in the night. The wounded outlaw had doubtless heard the sheriff talking and, the coast being clear to the southward, had got the fresh horse and was by that time probably safe in the heavy forests and mountains of Utah. His getting in with N'Yawk had been a daring ruse, but a successful one. Where his partner was, no one could guess. But by that time all the camp excepting Herman and Mrs. Louderer were so panicky that we couldn't have made a rational suggestion.

N'Yawk, white around his mouth, approached Mrs. Louderer. "I want to quit," he said. "Well," she said, calmly sipping her coffee, "you haf done it." "I'm sick," he stammered. "I know you iss," she said, "I haf before now seen men get sick when they iss scared to death." "My old daddy—" he began. "Yes, I know, he waded the creek vone time und you has had cold feet effer since."

Poor fellow, I felt sorry for him. I had cold feet myself just then, and I was

powerfully anxious
to warm them by my
own fire where a pair
of calm blue eyes
would reassure me.

I didn't get to see the
branding that was to
have taken place on
the range that day.
The boss insisted
on taking the trail
of his valued horse.
He was very angry.
He thought there
was a traitor among

the posse. Who started the firing at the bridge no one knew, and Watson said openly that it was done to get the sheriff away from camp.

My own home looked mighty good to me when we drove up that evening. I don't want any more wild life on the range,— not for a while, anyway.

Your ex-Washlady,
Elinore Rupert
Stewart.

XVII
AT GAVOTTE'S CAMP

November 16, 1912.
My dear Friend,—

At last I can write
you as I want to. I
am afraid you think
I am going to wait
until the "bairns"
are grown up before
writing to my friends,
but indeed I shall
not. I fully intend to
"gather roses while

I may." Since God has given me two blessings, children and friends, I shall enjoy them both as I go along.

I must tell you why I have not written as I should have done. All summer long my eyes were so strained and painful that I had to let all reading and writing go. And I have suffered terribly with my back. But now I am able to be about again, do most of my own work, and my eyes are much better. So now I shall not treat you so badly again. If you could only know how kind every one is to me, you would know that even ill health has its compensations out here. Dear Mrs. Louderer, with her goose-grease, her bread, and her delicious "kuchens." Mrs. O'Shaughnessy, with her cheery ways, her tireless friendship, and willing, capable hands. Gavotte even, with his tidbits of game and fish. Dear little Cora Belle came often to see me, sometimes bringing me a little of Grandpa's latest cure, which I received on faith, for, of course, I could not really swallow any of it. Zebbie's nephew, Parker Carter, came out, spent the summer with him, and they have now gone back to Yell County, leaving Gavotte in charge again.

Gavotte had a most interesting and prosperous

summer. He was commissioned by a wealthy Easterner to procure some fossils. I had had such a confined summer that Clyde took me out to Gavotte's camp as soon as I was able to sit up and be driven. We found him away over in the bad lands camped in a fine little grove. He is a charming man to visit at any time, and we found him in a particularly happy mood. He had just begun to quarry a gigantic find; he had piles of specimens; he had packed and shipped some rare specimens of fossil plants, but his "beeg find" came later and he was jubilant. To dig fossils successfully requires great care and knowledge, but

it is a work in which
Gavotte excels. He
is a splendid cook.
I almost believe he
could make a Johnny
Reb like codfish, and
that night we had
a delicious supper
and all the time
listening to a learned
discourse about
prehistoric things. I
enjoyed the meal and
I enjoyed the talk,
but I could not sleep
peacefully for being

chased in my dreams by pterodactyls, dinosaurs, and iguanodons, besides a great many horrible creatures whose names I have forgotten. Of course, when the ground begins to freeze and snow comes, fossil-mining is done for until summer comes, so Gavotte tends the critters and traps this winter. I shall not get to go to the mountains this winter. The babies are too small, but there is always some happy and interesting thing happening, and I shall have two pleasures each time, my own enjoyment, and getting to tell you of them.

XVIII
THE HOMESTEADER'S MARRIAGE AND A LITTLE FUNERAL

December 2, 1912.
Dear Mrs. Coney,—

Every time I get a new letter from you I get a new inspiration, and I am always glad to hear from you.

I have often wished I might tell you all about my Clyde, but have not because of two things. One is I could not even begin without telling you what a good man he is, and I didn't want you to think I could do nothing but brag. The other reason is the haste I married in. I am ashamed of that. I am afraid you will think me a Becky Sharp of a person. But although I married in haste,

I have no cause to repent. That is very fortunate because I have never had one bit of leisure to repent in. So I am lucky all around. The engagement was powerfully short because both agreed that the trend of events and ranch work seemed to require that we be married first and do our "sparking" afterward. You see, we had to chink in the wedding between times, that is, between planting the oats and other work that must be done early or not at all. In Wyoming ranchers can scarcely take time even to be married in the springtime. That having been settled, the license was sent for by mail, and as soon as it came Mr. Stewart saddled Chub and went down to the house of Mr. Pearson, the justice of the peace and a friend of long standing. I had never met any of the family and naturally rather dreaded to have them come, but Mr. Stewart was firm in wanting to be married at home, so he told Mr. Pearson he wanted him and his family to come up the following Wednesday and serve papers on the "wooman i' the hoose." They were astonished, of course, but being such good friends they promised him all the assistance they could render. They are quite the dearest, most interesting family! I have since learned to love them as my own.

Well, there was no time to make wedding clothes, so I had to "do up" what I did have. Isn't it queer how sometimes, do what you can, work will keep getting in the way until you can't get anything done? That is how it was with me those few days before the wedding; so much so that when Wednesday dawned everything was topsy-turvy and I had a very strong desire to run away. But I always did hate a "piker," so I stood pat. Well, I had most of the dinner cooked, but it kept me hustling to get the house into anything like decent order before the old dog barked, and I knew my moments of liberty were limited. It was blowing a perfect hurricane and snowing like midwinter. I had bought a beautiful pair of shoes to wear on that day, but my vanity had squeezed my feet a little, so while I was so busy at work I had kept on a worn old pair, intending to put on the new ones later; but when the Pearsons drove up all I thought about was getting them into the house where there was fire, so I forgot all about the old shoes and the apron I wore.

I had only been here six weeks then, and was a stranger. That is why I had no one to help me and was so confused and hurried. As soon as the newcomers were warm, Mr. Stewart told me I had better come over by him and stand up. It was a large room I had to cross, and how I did it before all those strange eyes I never knew. All I can remember very distinctly is hearing Mr. Stewart saying, "I will," and myself chiming in that I would, too. Happening to glance down, I saw that I had forgotten to take off my apron or my old shoes, but just then Mr. Pearson pronounced us man and wife, and as I had dinner to serve right away I had no time to worry over my odd toilet. Anyway the shoes were comfortable and the apron white, so I suppose it could have been worse; and I don't think it has ever made any difference with the Pearsons, for I number them all among my most esteemed friends.

It is customary here for newlyweds to give a dance and supper at the hall, but as I was a stranger I preferred not to, and so it was a long time before I became acquainted with all my neighbors. I had not thought I should ever marry again. Jerrine was always such a dear little pal, and I wanted to just knock about foot-loose and free to see life as a gypsy sees it. I had planned to see the Cliff-Dwellers' home; to live right there until I caught the spirit of the surroundings enough to live over their lives in imagination anyway. I had planned to see the old missions and to go to Alaska; to hunt in Canada. I even dreamed of Honolulu. Life stretched out before me one long, happy jaunt. I aimed to see all the world I could, but to travel unknown bypaths to do it. But first I wanted to try homesteading.

But for my having the grippe, I should never have come to Wyoming. Mrs. Seroise, who was a nurse at the institution for nurses in Denver while I was housekeeper there, had worked one summer at Saratoga,

Wyoming. It was she who told me of the pine forests. I had never seen a pine until I came to Colorado; so the idea of a home among the pines fascinated me. At that time I was hoping to pass the Civil-Service examination, with no very definite idea as to what I would do, but just to be improving my time

and opportunity.
I never went to a
public school a day
in my life. In my
childhood days there
was no such thing in
the Indian Territory
part of Oklahoma
where we lived, so I
have had to try hard
to keep learning.
Before the time came
for the examination
I was so discouraged
because of the grippe
that nothing but the

mountains, the pines, and the clean, fresh air seemed worth while; so it all came about just as I have written you.

So you see I was very deceitful. Do you remember, I wrote you of a little baby boy dying? That was my own little Jamie, our first little son. For a long time my heart was crushed. He was such a sweet, beautiful boy. I wanted him so much. He died of erysipelas. I held him in my arms till the last agony was over. Then I dressed the beautiful little body for the grave. Clyde is a carpenter; so I wanted him to make the little coffin. He did it every bit, and I lined and padded it, trimmed and covered it. Not that we couldn't afford to buy one or that our neighbors were not all that was kind and willing; but because it was a sad pleasure to do everything for our little first-born ourselves.

As there had been no physician to help, so there was no minister to comfort, and I could not bear to let our baby leave the world without leaving any message to a community that sadly needed it. His little message to us had been love, so I selected a chapter from John and we had a funeral service, at which all our neighbors for thirty miles around were present. So you see, our union is sealed by love and welded by a great sorrow.

Little Jamie was the first little Stewart. God has given me two more precious little sons. The old sorrow is not so keen now. I can bear to tell you about it, but I never could before. When you think of me, you must think of me as one who is truly happy. It is true, I want a great many things I haven't got, but I don't want them enough to be discontented and not enjoy the many blessings that are mine. I have my home among the blue mountains, my healthy, well-formed children, my clean, honest husband, my kind, gentle milk cows, my garden which I make myself. I have loads and loads of flowers which I tend myself. There are lots of chickens, turkeys, and pigs which are my own special care. I have some slow old gentle horses and an old wagon. I can load up the kiddies and go where I please any time. I have the best, kindest neighbors and I have my dear absent friends. Do you wonder I am so happy? When I think of it all, I wonder how I can crowd all my joy into one short life. I don't want you to think for one moment that you are bothering me when I write you. It is a real pleasure to do so. You're always so good to let me tell you everything. I am only afraid of trying your patience too far. Even in this long letter I can't tell you all I want to; so I shall write you again soon. Jerrine will write too. Just now she has very sore fingers. She has been picking gooseberries, and they have been pretty severe on her brown little paws.

With much love to you, I am

"Honest and truly" yours,

Elinore Rupert Stewart.

ABOUT THE AUTHOR

Elinore Pruitt Stewart was born on June 3rd, 1876 in White Bead Hill, which was then a settlement in Chickasaw Nation, Indian Territory, and is now in Oklahoma. She offers a window into her bold life with these adventurous letters, which were the basis for the 1979 film Heartland.

ABOUT THE COVER

The cover is adapted from an Untitled Pastoral Scene by the American painter, David Johnson from 1867.

WHAT WE'RE ABOUT

I started making Super Large Print books for my grandma. I wanted books that she could keep reading as her glaucoma and macular degeneration advanced. So I chose a font originally designed for people with dyslexia, because the letters are bold and easy to distinguish. It is set at 30 pt, nearly twice the size of traditional Large Print books.

Digital reading was too frustrating for my grandma. It could never offer the pleasures she had always associated with reading: the peacefulness of turning a page, the satisfaction in knowing a story has "this much left," and the comforting memories of adventure, companionship, and revelation she felt when seeing the cover of her favorite book. Part of what makes reading so relaxing and grounding is the tactile experience. I hope these books can bring joy to those who want to keep reading and to those who've never had the pleasure of curling up with a page turner.

Please let me know if these books are helpful to you and if you have any requests for new titles. To leave feedback and to see the complete and constantly updating catalog, please visit:

superlargeprint.com

MORE BOOKS AT:

superlargeprint.com

KEEP ON READING!

ISBN 9781077463486